Everywhere Beauty Is Harlem

The Vision of Photographer Roy DeCarava

GARY GOLIO

ART BY E. B. LEWIS

CALKINS CREEK
AN IMPRINT OF ASTRA BOOKS FOR YOUNG READERS
New York

It doesn't have to be pretty to be true,
but if it's true it's beautiful.
Truth is beautiful.

—Roy DeCarava

It's five o'clock. Work is over.
Roy's time is his own now.

On the subway, he pulls out a new roll
of film, opens the back of his camera, and
pops it in.

He's ready.

An old man sits across from him, dreaming.
Roy's dreaming, too—of all the treasures
he'll find.

Stepping into the light, Roy rubs his eyes.
They have to be wide open.
He'll be listening with them.

*I don't know where I'm going,
but I'm going!*

It's a warm summer day.
The air smells of french fries,
car smoke, and coffee.
Roy's hungry—but not for food.
His camera is hungry, too.

There's a boy on his hands and knees,
drawing chalk on the sidewalk.
He looks up and grins.

SNAP!

Roy keeps on walking.

An artist on the sidewalk is showing his paintings to a passerby.

A patch of light on the man's head catches Roy's attention.

Then it's gone.

Now it's Roy's turn to smile.

Down the street, in front
of a building, a woman is taking
pictures of her son with
a simple little camera.

Roy watches the boy, who's looking at his mother. There's a lot of love in those eyes.

SNAP!

They didn't even notice.

Beauty is not in the camera.
Beauty is in the person.

Roy feels like Superman.
Invisible rays come out of his eyes, scanning everything around him.
He sees so much beauty. Everywhere.
Does everyone have this power?

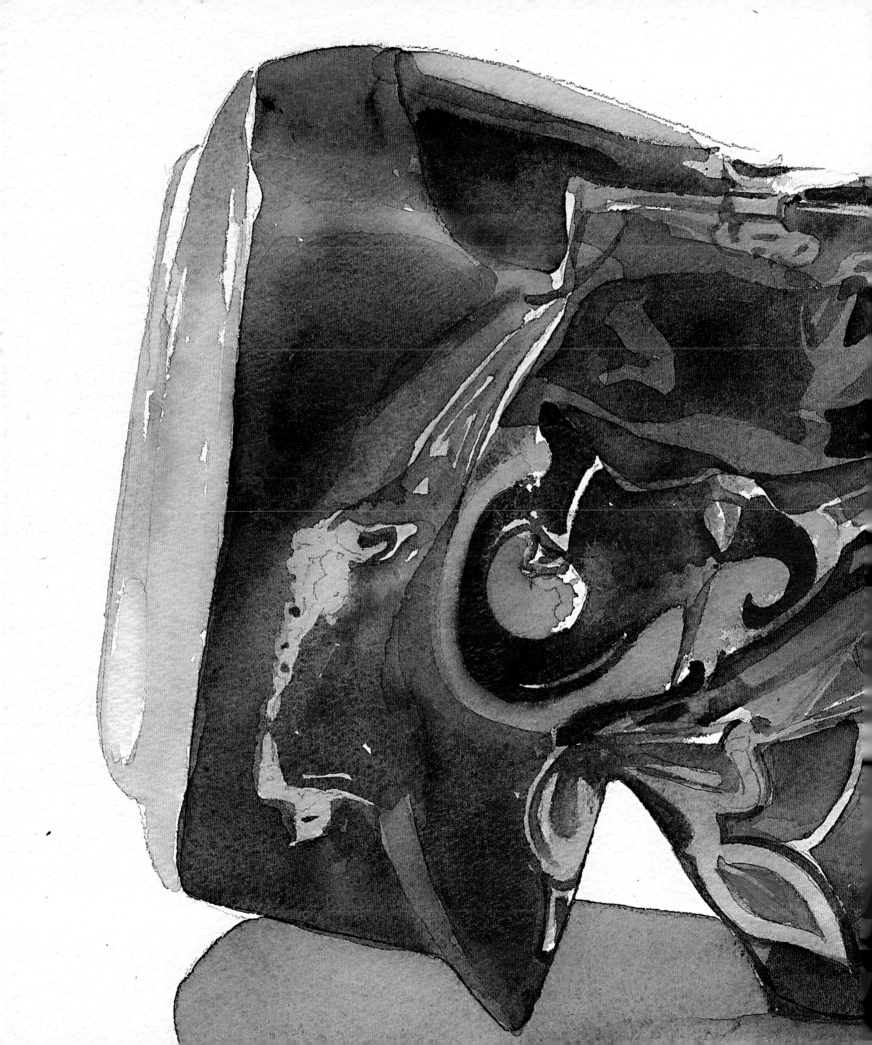

Lying at Roy's feet is an old crumpled soda can.

Close up, seen through the camera lens, it's *gigantic*—the size of a car!

SNAP!

Life is how you look at it.

A young man is standing at a bus stop,
a baby in his arms.

They're like one person.

Just as Roy is about to snap the shutter,
a bus pulls up, blocking his view.

That picture will have to stay in Roy's
mind—forever.

*I believe in patience, and knowledge,
and skill, and love.*

A *whoosh* of water shoots through
the air—a rainbow!
Older boys have opened a fire hydrant, and
they're playing in the spray.

SNAP!

Black and brown bodies,
shining bright in the light.

People are passing each other
on the street.
Some happy, some sad.
Their eyes are like mirrors.
Looking into them, Roy sees Harlem.

The sun's going down.
It's time to head home.
In front of a brick wall and
an empty lot, a young girl stands
in a long white dress.
Waiting.
Roy holds his breath.
For a moment, there's only
silence.

SNAP!

*We're looking for truth and truth is living,
so we find truth in living.*

Who Was Roy DeCarava?

You should be able to look at me and see my work. You should be able to look at my work and see me.

Roy Rudolph DeCarava was a child of Harlem, and the spirit of that place stayed with him all his life. As a child, he played in Harlem's streets—drawing chalk on the sidewalks and making jewelry out of what he found there. He went to Harlem movie houses on Sunday and fell in love with the black-and-white images on the big screen. To make money, Roy shined shoes, sold newspapers, and even delivered ice (at the time, not everyone had a refrigerator). He loved learning, from kindergarten on, especially when it came to art. His mother, a single parent, encouraged her son in music and drawing. As an amateur photographer, she set a powerful example by taking pictures of everything around her.

Inspired by the work of artist Vincent van Gogh, Roy initially wanted to be a painter himself. Eventually, he turned his eye to photography, and began taking his 35mm camera to the streets when he was in his twenties. While working many different jobs to support himself, Roy used his free time—on the subway, to and from home, in friends' houses and at jazz music clubs in Harlem—to record the beauty of what he saw around him. And he saw beauty everywhere. His photographs, noted for their dark, rich tones, were taken without flash, with only the light he found in a room or on the street. They're filled with a sense of the mystery seen in everyday things and ordinary people.

Roy became one of the most famous photographers of his time, and his mission was simple:

I try to photograph things that are near to me because I work best among things I know. My photographs are subjective and personal—they're intended to be accessible, to relate to people's lives. . . . People—their well-being and survival—are the crux of what's important to me.

I want to photograph Harlem through the Negro people. Morning, noon, night, at work, going to work, coming home from work, at play, in the streets, talking, kidding, laughing, in the home, in the playgrounds, in the schools, bars, stores, libraries, beauty parlors, churches, etc. . . . I want to show the strength, the wisdom, the dignity of the Negro people. Not the famous and the well known, but the unknown and the unnamed, thus revealing the roots from which spring the greatness of all human beings.

Seeing Everywhere Beauty

Roy DeCarava *loved* Harlem—its people, places, and different moods—and that love shows in his photos. If Roy had a message for us, it might be: *Look around at what you love where you live.* If you want to know what that feels like, take a cell phone, camera, or just a good set of eyes, and imagine you're seeing things around you for the first time. Most of all, look slowly.

Roy also let himself be surprised—by the way light falls on someone's face, a tree, an old crumpled-up soda can, or the shape of a child's shadow on the street. In fact, he and his camera *looked* for surprises wherever they went. So Roy's other message might be: *Unexpected treasures are waiting to be seen, if you just take the time to look.*

What I wanted to do was to give people a reason for being alive, a reason to feel good about themselves.

Portrait of Roy DeCarava by Anthony Barboza, 1974

Roy DeCarava's Life and Times

December 9, 1919—Roy is born in Harlem, New York, to a Jamaican mother and American father.

1924—Roy becomes a "chalk artist" at age five on Harlem sidewalks.

1920s–1930s—The Harlem Renaissance celebrates the flowering of Black American arts and culture.

1929–late 1930s—The Great Depression hits the United States, creating widespread economic hardship.

1934–38—Roy studies oil painting, inspired by the Dutch painter, Vincent Van Gogh.

1938—Roy graduates from the segregated Textile High School in New York City.

1938–40—Roy studies arts and architecture at the Cooper Union in New York City, but leaves because of ongoing racism at the school.

1940–42—Roy studies painting and printmaking at the Harlem Community Art Center.

1940s—Roy works for the Works Progress Administration, a Depression-era arts program, and begins photographing everyday life in Harlem.

December 7, 1941—Pearl Harbor, Hawaii, is bombed; the US enters World War II (1941–45).

1942—Roy is drafted into the army but honorably discharged after an "emotional breakdown."

Late 1940s on—Roy photographs jazz musicians at Harlem and other New York City clubs.

1950—Roy has his first exhibition of photos at the Forty-Fourth Street Gallery in New York City.

1952—Roy becomes the first Black American to receive the prestigious Guggenheim Fellowship, and spends a year photographing Harlem and its people.

1954—US Supreme Court decision *Brown v. Board of Education* paves the way for school desegregation.

1955—*The Sweet Flypaper of Life*, with Roy's photographs and words by Harlem poet Langston Hughes, is published.

1955—Roy's photos are shown in the historic *Family of Man* exhibition at the Museum of Modern Art, New York City.

Late 1950s–1975—Roy is a photographer for *Life*, *Newsweek*, *Sports Illustrated*, *Scientific American*, and other magazines.

1963—The March on Washington for Jobs and Freedom, where Martin Luther King Jr. delivers his "I Have A Dream" speech, takes place.

1964—The Civil Rights Act is passed, outlawing discrimination based on race or color.

1969—*Harlem on My Mind*, Roy's first museum exhibition, opens at the Metropolitan Museum of Art, New York City. Roy also joins protests outside the museum demanding greater inclusion of Black and Harlem artists.

1969–72—Roy becomes professor of art at the Cooper Union, New York City.

1971—Roy marries art historian Sherry Turner; they have three daughters.

1975—Roy becomes professor of art at Hunter College, New York City, a position he holds until 2009.

1970s on—Roy is honored with major photo exhibitions in the US and worldwide: Corcoran Gallery, Washington, DC; Studio Museum of Harlem, New York City; Art Institute of Chicago; international museums and collections.

1996—Roy is given a retrospective solo exhibition at the Museum of Modern Art, New York City.

2001—Roy publishes *The Sound I Saw*, images of jazz musicians and New York City.

2006—Roy receives the National Medal of Arts, the highest award given to US artists, from President George W. Bush.

October 27, 2009—Roy dies in Manhattan, New York City, at age 89.

The Argus A was Roy's first camera, a compact 35mm that he used to take his early and memorable shots of Harlem. SNAP!

Harlem apartment building in summer (1935–39), photographer unknown

Bibliography

The quotations used in this book can be found in the following sources marked with an asterisk (*).

DeCarava, Roy. *The Sound I Saw*. New York: Phaidon Press, 2001.

DeCarava, Roy, and Langston Hughes. *The Sweet Flypaper of Life*. New York: First Print Press, 2018.

*Galassi, Peter, and Sherry Turner DeCarava. *Roy DeCarava: A Retrospective*. New York: Museum of Modern Art, 1996.

*Hacking, Juliet. *Lives of the Great Photographers*. New York: Thames & Hudson, 2015.

Harris, Thomas Allen, dir. *Through A Lens Darkly*. First Run Features, 2015. DVD.

Kennedy, Randy. "Roy DeCarava, Harlem Insider Who Photographed Ordinary Life, Dies at 89." *New York Times*, October 28, 2009. nytimes. com/2009/10/29/arts/29decarava.html.

*"roy decarava 1." YouTube. August 14, 2014. Video, 6:51. youtube.com/watch?v=DNTbjVDfaVE.

"Roy DeCarava, Photographer Born." African American Registry. aaregistry.org/story/the-eyes-of-new-york-roy-decarava.

*"Roy DeCarava Tribute." Vimeo. 2011. Video, 20:40. vimeo.com/26581250.

*Scott, Dread. "An Interview with Roy DeCarava." A Gathering of the Tribes. tribes.org/web/2001/-06/24/an-interview-with-roy-decarava-by-dread-scott.

Willis, Deborah. *Reflections in Black: A History of Black Photographers, 1840 to the Present*. New York: W. W. Norton & Company, 2000.

Major Museums Featuring Roy's Photos

Roy DeCarava was an artist with a camera, who believed in the power of art to capture the spirit of life. He would have been delighted to see the spirit of his life captured by the masterful E. B. Lewis, an artist with a brush. To see Roy's photographs, visit the museums listed below or simply search online under his name.

Art Institute of Chicago, Illinois: artic.edu

Harvard Art Museums, Cambridge, Massachusetts: harvardartmuseums.org

Metropolitan Museum of Art, New York, New York: metmuseum.org

Museum of Fine Arts, Boston, Massachusetts: mfa.org

The Museum of Fine Arts, Houston, Texas: mfah.org

Museum of Modern Art, New York, New York: moma.org

National Gallery of Art, Washington, DC: nga.gov

Philadelphia Museum of Art, Pennsylvania: philamuseum.org

San Francisco Museum of Modern Art, California: sfmoma.org

Smithsonian American Art Museum, Washington, DC: americanart.si.edu

Picture Credits

To loving what we see. To seeing what
we love. —GG

To the visionaries of the Harlem
Renaissance —EBL

Calkins Creek
An imprint of Astra Books for Young Readers,
a division of Astra Publishing House
astrapublishinghouse.com
Printed in China

ISBN: 978-1-6626-8055-7 (hc)
ISBN: 978-1-6626-8056-4 (eBook)
Library of Congress Control Number: 2023905059

First edition
10 9 8 7 6 5 4 3 2 1

Design by Barbara Grzeslo
The text is set in ITC Legacy Sans Std medium.
The illustrations are done in watercolor on
Arches 300lb cold pressed paper.